EMBRACING GOD'S CALL

DAVID VUNDI

Alphy School Publishers
Wien, Österreich.

ISBN: 978-3-9505428-2-0 (Paperback)
ISBN: 978-3-9505428-3-7 (E-Book)

Alphy School
www.alphyschool.org, www.alphy.at
info@alphyschool.org

Printed in Austria
12 11 10 9 8 7 6 5 4

[18] Then Jesus came to them and said, "All authority in heaven and on earth has been given to me. [19] Therefore, go and make disciples of all nations, baptizing them in the name of the Father and of the Son and of the Holy Spirit, [20] and teaching them to obey everything I have commanded you. And surely, I am with you always, to the very end of the age."
Matthew 28:18-20

[19] Brethren, if anyone among you wanders from the truth, and someone turns him back, [20] let him know that he who turns a sinner from the error of his way will save a soul from death and cover a multitude of sins.
James 5:19-20

Those who are wise shall shine
Like the brightness of the firmament,
And those who turn many to righteousness
Like the stars forever and ever.
Daniel 12:3

Chapter 1
Introduction

I did not always understand the gospel, even though I grew up around it.

I was born and raised in a Christian family. Church and Scripture were familiar. Faith was part of my life. For a long time, I assumed that was enough. I believed, without ever saying it out loud, that because my parents were Christians, heaven would somehow be automatic for me as well.

But God, in His mercy, did not leave me in that misunderstanding.

In grade 9 of high school, something simple but life-changing happened. My brother sat down and shared the gospel with me, not as a debate, not as a lecture, but as truth spoken in love for his younger brother. For the first time, I understood that salvation is not inherited. I realized that I was born a sinner, that there was nothing good in me that could earn God's favor, and that faith could not be borrowed from anyone else.

That moment was painful, but it was also freeing.

I knelt and asked God for forgiveness, acknowledging all my sins. I remember numerous mistakes and sins from my childhood. My heart felt so light, filled with heavenly joy. I realized that salvation is personal, and I gave my heart to Jesus Christ.

From that day forward, everything changed.

Not all at once, and not perfectly, but profoundly. Faith was no longer something around me; it became alive within me. Jesus was no longer just a distant figure; He became **my Savior** and **my Lord.** And with that transformation came a strong desire I could not ignore. I wanted others to know Him, too.

I wanted everyone who had not yet encountered Christ to hear the same good news that had transformed my life.

Since then, I have often tried my best to live out Jesus' teachings perfectly and to share the gospel through both my words and my life. I have learned that following Christ is not about having all the answers, but about walking faithfully and pointing others to Him whenever the opportunity arises.

Yet alongside this joy, I have carried a growing sense of sadness.

I see many believers who genuinely love Jesus yet live quiet, passive lives when it comes to sharing their faith. They attend church, read Scripture, and pray, but rarely speak to anyone about the God who saved them, not out of rebellion, but out of comfort, fear, or habit.

And all around us, people are running toward destruction, living without the God who created them, without hope, without forgiveness, without eternal life.

This tension is what led me to write this book. Not anger. Not judgment. But love and urgency.

Hearing the Call Again

As you begin this journey through *Embracing God's Call*, you are not simply starting another Christian book. You are stepping into an invitation, an invitation to see your faith, your life, and your everyday relationships through a clearer and more purposeful lens.

The words Jesus spoke nearly two thousand years ago still echo today:

"Go therefore and make disciples of all the nations." (Matthew 28:19, NKJV)

These words were never meant to feel distant or reserved for a select few. They spoke to ordinary believers, men and women who would return to daily life, work, and relationships. They were spoken for every generation. And they were spoken for you.

The command to make disciples is an ongoing process, not a single moment. It is a living call that continues to shape the Church today. This book exists to help you rediscover that call not as a burden but as a privilege; not as something that pulls you away from daily life but as something that gives daily life eternal meaning.

This is not an academic study or a theoretical discussion. It is a call to action. A call to awareness. A call to faithful obedience.

A World at Our Doorstep

We are living in a unique moment in human history. Never before have so many cultures, languages, and nations lived side by side. International migration, global business, and education have transformed our cities and neighborhoods.

People from *all nations* are no longer far away. They are our coworkers, classmates, neighbors, and friends.

Jesus' command to "go" does not always require a passport. Often, it involves something much closer to home: awareness, intentionality, and love.

In workplaces, schools, and communities around the world, believers interact daily with people who have never clearly heard the gospel. Children sit next to classmates from different faith backgrounds. Offices and companies bring together people from many nations and languages.
The mission field is no longer distant. It is right at our doorstep.

This reality removes one of the most common excuses Christians make: *"I'm not called to missions."*
If you are a believer living among people who do not yet know Christ, then you are already on the mission field.

The question is not whether you are called. The question is how you will live out the calling God has placed on your life.

The Urgency of Love

Jesus once said:

"The harvest truly is plentiful, but the laborers are few." (Matthew 9:37, NKJV)

Those words remain true today. Beneath success, education, and material comfort, many people are quietly asking the same questions humanity has always asked: *Why am I here? Is there hope beyond this life? Who is God?*

Sharing the gospel is urgent, not because we want to win arguments, but because we love people. We do not have much time, and opportunities pass quickly. Conversations that feel ordinary today may never happen again.

Every believer is a steward of time, relationships, and influence. How we use these gifts matters eternally.

Never Sent Alone

Yet Jesus does not send us out alone. He concludes the Great Commission with a promise that changes everything:

"And surely I am with you always, to the very end of the age." (Matthew 28:20, NKJV)

Our calling does not depend on our confidence, eloquence, or strength. It depends on God's presence. The Father sends, The Son leads, and The Holy Spirit empowers.

The commission to make disciples is not a burden placed on human shoulders; it is a divine partnership.

And this book is an invitation to step into it.

William Carey and an ordinary beginning

To understand how God uses ordinary people to achieve extraordinary things, consider the life of William Carey (1761–1834). He is often called "the father of modern missions." You can read more about him in my first book in this series, "Missionaries Who Changed the World".

He was not a famous preacher or church leader when God stirred his heart for the nations. He was a simple shoemaker in England. While repairing shoes, he taught himself geography and languages by reading about distant lands and their inhabitants. As he studied Scripture, he realized that Jesus's command to make disciples of all nations was still in effect.

At the time, many Christians believed that the commission to make disciples applied only to the original apostles. Carey disagreed. He famously argued that if Jesus commanded His disciples to teach others to obey everything He commanded, then this responsibility must continue from generation to generation.

Despite resistance and criticism, and with limited resources, Carey traveled to India in 1793. His early years there were marked by hardship, poverty, illness, the death of a child, and years without visible results. Yet he persevered. Over time, he translated the Bible into multiple Indian languages, faithfully preached the Gospel, and helped lay the foundation for education and social reform.

What makes Carey's story especially meaningful is not his eventual success but his humble beginnings. He did not start as a missionary hero. He began as an ordinary believer who took Jesus's words seriously. His life reminds us that obedience often starts quietly, long before visible results appear.

One of the most important changes believers need to make is viewing sharing the Gospel not as an occasional activity but as a way of life. Mission isn't something we schedule; it's something we live.

This book is not about traditional missionary methods, strategies, or programs. There are already many excellent resources on those topics. Instead, this book is about viewing everyday life through the lens of Jesus's command, "*Go and make disciples.*"

Teachers shape young minds every day. Doctors and nurses care for bodies. Taxi drivers hear the stories of countless passengers. Business professionals influence workplace culture. Parents discipline their children at home. Students build friendships across cultures. Each of these roles is important in God's kingdom. When approached intentionally and with love, these roles provide sacred spaces where the gospel can be shared naturally and authentically.

You don't need to leave your profession to be a missionary. In many cases, your profession is the very platform God intends to use.

As I said before, the commission to make disciples is urgent yet joyful. It feels good to know that our lives matter to others. It is an honor to be part of God's plan to save people.

As a believer, you are invited to participate in the most important story ever told. This is the truth about God's decision to forgive the world through Jesus Christ's sacrifice on the cross.

This journey will undoubtedly have its challenges. There will be fear, resistance, misunderstandings, and discouraging moments. But there will also be moments of pure joy when you have meaningful conversations and see your prayers being answered. When you see people coming to the Lord, your faith will grow stronger, too.

As you read this book, I encourage you to think, rethink, and respond. If you have never shared the good news of the Gospel of Jesus Christ with anyone, consider this a personal invitation. View the mission as the calling of every believer, not something reserved for a select few. My dear brother and sister, I humbly ask you to step outside your comfort zone, interact with others in loving, humble ways, and trust that God can accomplish great things through your faith every day.

The commission to make disciples is both an invitation and a command. It is an invitation to follow Jesus. It is an invitation to live with purpose. It is a call to share God's love with the world.

Let's start this journey together. We should accept God's call in the present moment, not in the future or elsewhere. The world is waiting, and by God's grace, you are a missionary.

Questions for reflection
1. How has your personal encounter with the Great Commission been?
2. How do you see the urgency of the Great Commission in today's world?

3. What steps can you take to respond more fully to God's call in your life?

Prayer

Dear Heavenly Father, thank You for calling me to participate in Your mission. Please help me to see the urgency of the commission to make disciples and to embrace it wholeheartedly. Fill me with Your Spirit and guide me as I seek to make disciples of all nations. In Jesus' name, I pray. Amen.

Chapter 2

Go, *make disciples of all nations*

In the previous chapter, we reflected on how God calls people personally, often through simple, ordinary moments, to awaken them to the truth of the gospel. That personal call, however, is never meant to stop with us. From the very beginning, God's work in a person's life is meant to overflow into the lives of others.

This is where the Great Commission comes into focus.

Few passages in Scripture are as well-known as Jesus' final words to His disciples. Yet familiarity does not always lead to understanding. Many believers can quote the command to "*go and make disciples of all nations*," but far fewer have paused to consider what Jesus truly meant or what those words require of us today.

"*Go therefore and make disciples of all the nations, baptizing them in the name of the Father and of the Son and of the Holy Spirit, teaching them to observe all things that I have commanded you;*

and lo, I am with you always, even to the end of the age." (Matthew 28:19–20, NKJV)

At first glance, the command may seem straightforward. Yet after years of church life and ministry, it becomes clear that while some believers grasp its depth, many misunderstand it or unintentionally reduce it.

Jesus gives us two key phrases that deserve careful attention: **"go and make disciples"** and **"of all nations."** When we understand these clearly, the Great Commission becomes less confusing and far more personal.

More Than Making Converts

For many decades, the phrase *"make disciples"* has often been understood as *"make converts."* In other words, share the gospel so that unbelievers come to faith in Jesus Christ. This understanding is not wrong, but it is incomplete.

Evangelism is essential. People must hear the gospel. They must respond in faith. They must be baptized and welcomed into the fellowship of the Church. All of this belongs to the first and necessary phase of disciple-making.

But Jesus does not stop there.

He continues:

"and teaching them to obey everything I have commanded you. And surely I am with you always, to the very end of the age." (Matthew 28:20, NKJV)

This second phase, which involves teaching believers how to live according to Jesus's teachings, has often been overlooked. However, it is central to the concept of discipleship.

To make disciples is not only to introduce people to Christ, but to help them grow into Christlikeness. It is a lifelong process of learning, obedience, and transformation.

Jesus' Model of Disciple-Making

Jesus Himself shows us how disciples are formed. He did not rely on sermons alone. He gathered a small group of followers and invited them to walk closely with Him. They learned through teaching, conversation, correction, example, and practice.

His approach included:
- Teaching in large groups
- Explaining truth in smaller gatherings
- Personal conversations and guidance
- Real-life application and correction

The goal was not information, but transformation.

Over time, as His disciples absorbed His words and acted on them with faith and love, they began to reflect His character. This process did not happen overnight. It was the work of a lifetime. The apostle Paul understood this deeply. He urged believers,

"Imitate me, just as I also imitate Christ."
(1 Corinthians 11:1, NKJV)

And he described his ministry this way,

"*Him we preach, warning every man and teaching every man in all wisdom, that we may present every man perfect in Christ Jesus. To this end, I also labor, striving according to His working which works in me mightily.*" (Colossians 1:28–29, NKJV)

Disciple-making is not casual or shallow. It is a labor of love.

Where the Church Has Struggled

One of the greatest weaknesses in the modern Church is not a lack of activity, but a lack of maturity. Many believers remain spiritually immature, entangled in sin, shaped more by culture than by Christ.

This is not merely an individual problem; it is a discipleship problem.

Teaching from the pulpit is essential. Small groups are essential. But discipleship also requires personal relationships, older believers walking patiently with younger believers, helping them apply Jesus' teachings to real life.

This kind of discipleship takes time. It may feel impossible in large churches, but it is not. When disciple-making becomes a shared responsibility rather than a task reserved for pastors, a culture of growth can slowly take root.

God delights in this work. And He empowers those who make it a priority.

"Of All Nations"

The second phrase Jesus uses, *"of all nations"*, expands the scope of the mission beyond anything His disciples had known before.

Scripture teaches that humanity shares a common origin, even though we have developed into many ethnic and cultural groups (Genesis 1:26–28; Acts 17:26). When Jesus speaks of "all nations," He is speaking of all peoples, every ethnic group, culture, and language.

This was a dramatic expansion of His earlier focus on *"the lost sheep of the house of Israel"* (Matthew 10:6).

Although Jesus' earthly ministry was primarily among the Jews, He consistently hinted at a broader mission. His interaction with the Samaritans revealed God's heart for those beyond Israel. He spoke of *"other sheep"* who would one day be gathered into one flock (John 10:16).

The Mission Unfolds

After Jesus' ascension, this global mission begins to unfold clearly.

"But you shall receive power when the Holy Spirit has come upon you; and you shall be witnesses to Me in Jerusalem, and in all Judea and Samaria, and to the end of the earth." (Acts 1:8, NKJV)

The book of Acts shows this progression beautifully:

- Jerusalem (Acts 2–7)
- Samaria (Acts 8)
- The Ethiopian official carrying the gospel to Africa (Acts 8:26–38)
- Paul's missionary journeys throughout the Roman world (Acts 13–28)

God's mission moves steadily outward, crossing cultural and geographic boundaries.

A Vision of the End

Scripture also gives us a glimpse of where this mission is heading:

"After these things I looked, and behold, a great multitude which no one could number, of all nations, tribes, peoples, and tongues, standing before the throne and before the Lamb." (Revelation 7:9–10, NKJV)

This is God's redeemed family, diverse and united, worshiping together.

Our Personal Response

How, then, should we respond?

The first step is commitment to share the gospel with anyone and everyone, regardless of background, and to help believers grow in Christ. Many Christians hesitate here. Some believe they lack the gift of evangelism. Others feel unqualified to teach.

But Scripture does not call every believer to be an evangelist. It calls every believer to be a **witness** to share what Christ has done, what Jesus means to us, and the hope we have found in Him.

You do not need formal training to walk alongside someone else. Any believer who is growing in Christ can help another take their next step, provided they are willing to obey what they already know.

If this calling feels daunting, take comfort: it felt daunting to the first disciples as well. And to them and to us Jesus gives the same promise:

"I am with you always, even to the end of the age." (Matthew 28:20, NKJV)

The grace of our Lord Jesus Christ, the love of God the Father, and the fellowship of the Holy Spirit go with us every step of the way.

Questions for reflection

1. What do you think it truly means to follow Jesus in your everyday life, not just at church, but at home, work, or online?

2. In what areas of your life are you growing spiritually? Is there something God may be asking you to address or change?

3. Is there someone around you who could benefit from encouragement or guidance? What is one small step you could take?

4. Are there people you find difficult to understand or love? How can you ask God to help you see them with compassion?

Prayer

Lord, shape our hearts to truly follow You, not only in words, but in the way we live each day. Teach us to grow in obedience, humility, and love. Help us walk patiently with others as You continue to shape us. Open our eyes to see people as You see them and give us courage to live out our faith with sincerity and compassion. We trust that You are with us as we take each step forward. Amen.

Chapter 3
Awakened from Passive Faith
Why Silence is Not Love

For many believers, faith begins with joy. We remember accepting Jesus as Lord and Savior and experiencing the personal impact of the gospel, God's forgiveness and grace becoming real, and hope replacing fear. In those early days, talking about Jesus felt natural. Our hearts overflowed with these changes, and we spoke not out of obligation, but out of joy.

I still remember those days. I woke up each morning eager to tell someone about Jesus. My mind was constantly thinking and planning how to share this good news with all my college friends. In fact, even today, my heart remains the same. I long to bring more and more people to God. That is why I am writing this book to encourage my brothers and sisters in Christ to make disciples.

However, many Christians experience a gradual change over time.

We have a sincere faith in Jesus, but it grows quieter. Our belief stays strong, but our expression of it fades. Without any deliberate decision, faith turns inwards. Although we continue to attend church, read Scripture, and pray, sharing the gospel becomes rare and difficult. This is not because we no longer care, but because life becomes busy, routines settle in, and silence feels easier.

This quiet drift into passive faith is one of the most subtle challenges facing the Church today. Most believers do not intentionally choose to be silent. It develops gradually. There may be many reasons for this. We may begin to feel that faith is a personal matter or that someone else is better equipped to explain the gospel. Over time, what once felt like courage slowly gives way to the desire for comfort.

Yet Scripture gently, and sometimes firmly, reminds us that faith was never meant to be hidden away.

Faith was never meant to be private

Faith was never meant to be private.

Jesus did not call His followers to simply believe in Him privately. From the beginning, he invited them to participate. When he said, 'Follow *me'*, he immediately added, *'and I will make you fishers of men'* (*Matthew* 4:19, NKJV). Discipleship and witness were never separate.

To follow Jesus is to share His passion for people.

This does not mean that every believer is called to public preaching or formal ministry. However, it does mean that, by its very nature, faith moves outward. Faith that never speaks, never points, and never invites is not the faith Jesus described.

Jesus Himself said:

"*Nor do they light a lamp and put it under a basket, but on a lampstand, and it gives light to all who are in the house.*" (*Matthew* 5:15, NKJV)

Hidden light may still exist, but it no longer serves its purpose.

You are the light of the world. Shine your light on others. Show them, Jesus, through your life.

When Silence Feels Like Kindness

Many Christians sincerely love God and care deeply about people, yet rarely speak about Christ. Often, this silence is justified as kindness. We tell ourselves that we do not want to offend, pressure, or harm relationships. These concerns are understandable, especially in a world that increasingly treats faith as a private matter.
But Scripture presents love differently.

Paul asks a direct and sobering question:

"How then shall they call on Him in whom they have not believed? And how shall they believe in Him of whom they have not heard?" (Romans 10:14, NKJV)

This verse does not accuse; it clarifies. Hearing is essential. As Romans 10:17 reminds us, faith comes by hearing. A Christlike life is powerful, but Scripture never suggests that example alone replaces explanation.

Silence may feel respectful, but biblical love always seeks the eternal good of others.

Jude writes with striking urgency:

"Save others by snatching them from the fire." (Jude 1:23, NKJV)

This is not harsh language; it is the language of rescue. When danger is real, love speaks. If so many are on their way toward eternal separation from God, how can we, as believers, remain silent and withhold the good news from them?

The comfort that lulls us to sleep

Many believers today live in environments that are free, safe, and stable. These are genuine gifts from God. However, comfort carries a subtle risk: it can dull our spiritual awareness.

Jesus repeatedly warned His disciples against spiritual complacency. He urged them to watch and remain alert. He said that salt that loses its flavor becomes ineffective (Matthew 5:13). If we are not careful, comfort can slowly erode our sense of urgency.

I see many believers in this generation choosing to remain quiet. As the title of this chapter suggests, I would describe them as passive, quiet at home, quiet at church, and even quiet in the workplace.

Peter echoes this warning with clarity:

"Be sober, be vigilant; because your adversary the devil walks about like a roaring lion, seeking whom he may devour." (1 Peter 5:8, NKJV)

At the same time, Scripture reminds us of the enemy's urgency:

"The devil has come down to you, having great wrath, because he knows that he has a short time." (Revelation 12:12, NKJV)

While believers may grow passive, Scripture tells us the enemy does not. This is not meant to produce fear, but to cultivate awareness. Time matters. Lives matter. Silence has consequences.

The Compassion of Christ

Jesus never separated love from truth. When He looked at crowds, He did not see interruptions. He saw people.

"But when He saw the multitudes, He was moved with compassion for them, because they

were weary and scattered, like sheep having no shepherd." (Matthew 9:36, NKJV)

Compassion moved Jesus to act.

He taught, healed, invited, and confronted not out of harshness, but out of love. He wept over Jerusalem, not because He was rejected, but because people were lost:

"Now as He drew near, He saw the city and wept over it." (Luke 19:41, NKJV)

Those tears reveal the heart of God: deep love paired with deep urgency. Jesus spoke truth gently, personally, and clearly. He never forced belief, but He never withheld the invitation.

Charles Spurgeon and the Weight of Silence

One Christian leader who understood this tension well was **Charles Haddon Spurgeon** (1834–1892). Known for his preaching, Spurgeon also believed deeply in personal witness. He often reminded believers that the gospel was entrusted to the whole Church, not just its leaders.

Spurgeon once remarked that if people were lost, Christians should at least ensure they had been warned. His words were not born out of judgment, but out of love for souls and reverence for God.

What made Spurgeon's ministry powerful was not merely eloquence, but conviction. He believed silence in the face of eternal reality was too heavy to carry. Love compelled him to speak.

Fear, Faith, and Honest Obedience

One of the greatest barriers to sharing Christ is fear of rejection, fear of saying the wrong thing, fear of being misunderstood.
Paul addressed this directly:

"For God has not given us a spirit of fear, but of power and of love and of a sound mind." (2 Timothy 1:7, NKJV)

God does not ask us to be fearless. He asks us to be faithful.
Sharing the gospel does not require perfect words or theological mastery. Often, it begins with honesty. The man healed by Jesus put it simply:

"One thing I know: that though I was blind, now I see." (John 9:25, NKJV)

Faith that fills the heart eventually finds its way to the lips.

True love means being willing to place others' eternal good above our temporary comfort. Parents warn children of danger. Doctors deliver difficult diagnoses. In the same way, believers speak of Christ not to win arguments, but to offer hope.

Paul expressed this burden clearly:

"Knowing, therefore, the terror of the Lord, we persuade men." (2 Corinthians 5:11, NKJV)

This was not manipulation, but compassion shaped by truth.

An Invitation, Not Condemnation

This chapter is not written to shame believers who struggle with fear or hesitation. Many faithful Christians desire to speak but feel unsure how to begin. The call here is not condemnation but awakening.

Faith was never meant to remain passive. Love was never meant to remain silent.

God has placed each believer in specific relationships, workplaces, and communities for a reason. These are not accidents. They are sacred opportunities.

Every believer is a missionary not because they are bold or trained, but because they are sent.

As we awaken from passive faith, may we learn to speak with humility, live with integrity, and love courageously, trusting that God will use even our smallest acts of obedience for His greater purposes.

Questions for reflection

1. In what ways has your faith become quieter over time, even though your belief in Christ remains sincere?

2. What fears or assumptions most often keep you silent about your faith?
3. How do you usually define love toward non-believers, and how does Scripture challenge or expand that definition?
4. Are there people in your life whom God may be prompting you to care for more intentionally?
5. What would it look like to take one small step from passive faith toward faithful obedience?

Prayer

Lord Jesus, thank You for saving us by Your grace and calling us to walk with You. Forgive us for the times we have allowed comfort, fear, or distraction to quiet our witness. Awaken our hearts again with compassion for those around us. Teach us to love as You love to speak truth with humility, courage, and grace. Help us trust You with the outcome as we take small steps of obedience. We place ourselves in Your hands once more, asking You to use our lives for Your glory. Amen.

Chapter 4
Living with Eternal urgency in a Perishing world

There is something about time that quietly shapes the way we live.

When we believe we have plenty of time, we tend to move slowly. We postpone many things, assuming we can deal with them later or the next day. We delay difficult conversations, procrastinate, and assume that there will always be another opportunity. But when we become aware that time is limited, everything changes. Our priorities change for sure. Our words carry greater weight. Our choices become more careful and intentional.

Scripture consistently calls believers to live with this kind of awareness, not fear, but clarity, not anxiety, but purpose. From beginning to end, the Bible reminds us that this world, as we know it, is temporary and that eternity is closer than we often realize.

For many Christians today, faith remains sincere, but the sense of urgency has faded. This is not because we doubt the gospel, but because daily life feels stable. Work schedules, family responsibilities, and familiar routines quietly push eternal matters into the background. Without realizing it, we begin to live as though there will always be more time.

I am often surprised by how many years I have already lived. Yet I remain aware that my time on earth is limited, and that I must do something for God before it is too late. Therefore, I seek to take every opportunity to speak about Jesus.

And yet, Scripture gently interrupts our assumption that there will always be tomorrow.

Seeing the World Through an Eternal Lens

The Bible never asks believers to live in fear, but it does call us to live awake. Life is described as brief yet meaningful, fragile yet sacred.

James writes:

"For what is your life? It is even a vapor that appears for a little time and then vanishes away." (James 4:14, NKJV)

This truth is not meant to frighten us; it is meant to refocus us. When we remember that life is short, our view of people, conversations, opportunities, and time changes.

Revelation offers a sobering reminder of the spiritual reality around us:

"The devil has come down to you, having great wrath, because he knows that he has a short time." (Revelation 12:12, NKJV)

Although believers may become complacent, Scripture tells us that the enemy does not. This is not a call to panic, but rather, to be aware. Time is limited, and spiritual realities are real.

Peter echoes this warning with pastoral clarity:

"Be sober, be vigilant; because your adversary the devil walks about like a roaring lion, seeking whom he may devour." (1 Peter 5:8, NKJV)

Being sober-minded means living attentively and recognizing the eternal significance of our lives.

Comfort and the Quiet Loss of Urgency

For believers living in peaceful and prosperous environments, one of the greatest challenges is comfort. Although comfort is a gift from God, it poses a subtle danger. When life feels predictable and safe, spiritual sensitivity can be dull.

I have a friend who watches videos about predicting the future all the time. These videos cover topics such as the economy, wars, and earthquakes. The sad thing is that he believes in everything he sees and tries to plan for a comfortable life. He is a Christian, yet he has lost his spiritual sensitivity and is not working hard enough to bring others to Christ.

Jesus often addressed this tendency. In Luke 12, for example, Jesus tells the story of a man who planned carefully for the future by storing up wealth and security.

God's response was direct:

"Fool! This night your soul will be required of you." (Luke 12:20, NKJV)

The problem was not planning; it was living without reference to eternity.

When believers lose sight of eternity, their faith slowly turns inward. We start asking, "Am I comfortable?" instead of "Am I faithful?" We stop asking how our lives intersect with God's mission, assuming that someone else will take responsibility.

Yet, Scripture consistently reminds us that the gospel was entrusted not only to leaders and missionaries but also to ordinary believers.

Jesus and the Compassion That Creates Urgency

Jesus Himself lived with a deep awareness of time. He was never rushed, yet He never wasted a moment. His life was marked by calm purpose and intentional love.

When He looked at the crowds, Scripture tells us:

"He was moved with compassion for them, because they were weary and scattered, like sheep having no shepherd." (Matthew 9:36, NKJV)

Compassion was the source of His urgency.

Immediately after this, Jesus said:

"The harvest truly is plentiful, but the laborers are few." (Matthew 9:37, NKJV)

The harvest was already ready. The need already existed. The challenge was participation.

Jesus did not say the harvest would be ready someday. He said it *was* ready. Eternal urgency grows when we realize that the people around us are already searching, hurting, and in need of hope.

Biblical urgency is never frantic. God does not rush His people, but He does invite them to respond.

Paul explains his own urgency this way:

"Knowing, therefore, the terror of the Lord, we persuade men." (2 Corinthians 5:11, NKJV)

This was not manipulation. Rather, it flowed from reverence for God and love for people.

Just a few verses later, Paul reveals the deeper motivation.

"For the love of Christ compels us." (2 Corinthians 5:14, NKJV)

The urgency born of love is patient, gentle, and sincere, but it does not remain silent.

Dwight L. Moody

Dwight L. Moody (1837–1899) lived with an awareness of eternity. Though he was neither a trained theologian nor a polished speaker, God used him powerfully because he believed that eternity mattered.

Moody said he wanted everyone he met to hear about Christ. It was not pressure; it was love. He believed that withholding the gospel posed a greater risk.

His urgency did not make him anxious. It made him faithful. He trusted God with the results, yet he refused to waste opportunities.

Moody's life reminds us that urgency does not require extraordinary ability, only sincere obedience.

Why We Postpone What Matters Most

Many believers assume that there will always be another chance. Another conversation. Another season.

However, scripture gently warns against that assumption:

"Today, if you will hear His voice, do not harden your hearts." (Hebrews 3:15, NKJV)

Urgency teaches us to value today.

The Holy Spirit often quietly prompts us to speak, pray, and reach out. When we repeatedly delay, those promptings become easier to ignore.

Eternal urgency invites us to respond while the opportunity is present.

When eternity becomes real, people stop being interrupted and start becoming invitations. Our colleagues, neighbors, and family members are not just part of our routine; they are souls deeply loved by God.

Paul describes this mindset shift clearly:

Paul describes this shift clearly:

"Therefore, from now on, we regard no one according to the flesh." (2 Corinthians 5:16, NKJV)

An eternal perspective reshapes how we see others, altering our perception of them and the relationships we have with them.

Watching, Waiting, and Living Ready

Jesus often warned His disciples to stay awake, not physically, but spiritually:

"Watch therefore, for you do not know what hour your Lord is coming." (Matthew 24:42, NKJV)

To watch is to live attentively, to remain prayerful and compassionate, and to be responsive to God's guidance.

Living with eternal urgency does not mean abandoning joy or rest. It means holding life with open hands, ready to respond when God opens a door.

Scripture never calls believers to measure success by visible results. It calls us to faithfulness:

"Moreover it is required in stewards that one be found faithful." (1 Corinthians 4:2, NKJV)

Some seeds take time to grow. Some conversations bear fruit years later. God sees what we cannot.

A Gentle Invitation to Live Differently

Living with eternal urgency changes the way we pray, listen, and speak. Rather than overwhelming us, it refocuses us.

If the gospel is true, then eternity matters.

If eternity matters, then lives matter.

If lives matter, then silence is never neutral.

Every believer is a missionary, not because time is running out, but because each day is a gift entrusted to us.

As we learn to live with eternal urgency, may our hearts remain tender, our eyes open, and our lives ready until Christ returns.

Reflection Questions

1. How often do you think about eternity in your daily life? How does this perspective influence your choices?
2. How has comfort or routine dulled your sense of spiritual urgency?

3. Are there people around you whom God may be inviting you to see with renewed compassion?
4. When have you felt the Holy Spirit prompting you to speak or act, but hesitated or delayed?
5. How would you live more intentionally without fear and with purpose in this season of your life?

Prayer

Gracious Lord, we thank You for the gift of each day and the hope of eternity through Jesus Christ. Forgive us for the times we lived distracted, assuming there would always be another opportunity. Awaken our hearts to compassion for those around us and help us to see life through Your eyes. Teach us to live with purpose, patience, and faithfulness, trusting You with the outcome. Use our time, words, and lives for Your glory. Until the day we see You face-to-face, help us live in readiness and obedience. In Jesus' name, Amen.

Chapter 5

Loving Enough to Speak
Sharing Christ with Family and Friends

In the previous chapter, we reflected on the urgency of eternity and the fleeting nature of time. Scripture reminded us that life is fragile, opportunities are limited, and love does not delay what matters most. However, as soon as believers start to take this urgency seriously, a new challenge often emerges: where do we begin?

For many Christians, the answer is both clear and challenging.

The hardest place to live out the Great Commission is not overseas or across cultures, but right at home. It's usually easier to talk about Jesus to strangers than to those who know us well, those who remember our past, share our history, and see our flaws firsthand.

Family members and close friends hold a special place in our lives. We care deeply about them and seek peace and harmony in these bonds. Because of this, many believers experience a quiet tension: a sincere desire for their loved ones to know Christ, combined with a deep fear of saying the wrong thing or creating distance.

This tension is not new. Scripture honestly acknowledges it and gently guides us forward, not with pressure, but with wisdom, prayer, and love.

God's Design for Faith to Flow Through Relationships

From the beginning, God has often chosen to work through families and close relationships. While salvation is always personal, it frequently spreads through connections with others. The Philippian jailer cried out in desperation, and Paul responded with words that offered hope beyond just the individual.

"Believe on the Lord Jesus Christ, and you will be saved, you and your household." (Acts 16:31, NKJV)

This was not a promise of automatic salvation, but an invitation. God's heart has always been to reach households, not just individuals.

Our closeness to family and friends provides us with opportunities unavailable to others. We share meals, celebrations, grief, and daily life.

Over time, these shared experiences build trust—and trust allows for meaningful conversations.

Why Speaking Feels So Difficult

Despite this closeness, many believers hesitate to discuss their faith with loved ones. The reasons are very human:

• Fear of rejection or misunderstanding

• A wish to avoid conflict or awkward moments

• Concern about being seen as judgmental

• Awareness of their own past mistakes

In these situations, silence often seems like the safest choice.

Jesus spoke honestly about this reality:

"A prophet is not without honor except in his own country, among his own relatives, and in his own house." (Mark 6:4, NKJV)

Jesus understood that familiarity can lead to resistance. Still, He did not exclude family from His mission; He included them. The real challenge is not whether we love our family and friends, but how we show that love.

Love Defined by Truth

In today's world, love is often described as acceptance without conditions. But Scripture shows love as something deeper and more meaningful.

Paul writes:

"Love rejoices in the truth." (1 Corinthians 13:6, NKJV)

If truth leads to life, then love cannot stay silent forever. Jude uses strong yet compassionate language when he urges believers to:

"Save others by snatching them from the fire." (Jude 1:23, NKJV)

This imagery isn't meant to scare us but to remind us that love often takes courage. Biblical love aims for the eternal good of others even when that means having difficult conversations.

Jesus Sends the Healed Man Home

One of the most memorable moments in the Gospels happens after Jesus frees a man from severe demon possession. Filled with gratitude, the man wants to follow Jesus. But Jesus gives an unexpected response:

"Go home to your friends and tell them what great things the Lord has done for you, and how He has had compassion on you." (Mark 5:19, NKJV)

Jesus sent him back to the place where his testimony would be most personal and most difficult.

The man was not sent with theological arguments, but with a story: what the Lord had done for him. His changed life and honest testimony became the message.

Monica and Augustine: Loving and Waiting

One of the most heartfelt examples of faithful love is found in Monica, the mother of Augustine of Hippo. Augustine was far from God for many years, chasing after pleasure and ambition while rejecting his mother's faith. Monica did not argue endlessly or retreat in bitterness. Instead, she prayed persistently. She spoke truth patiently. She consistently lived her faith.

Augustine later wrote that his mother's tears and prayers followed him everywhere. In time, God answered her prayers. Augustine surrendered his life to Christ and became one of the most influential Christian thinkers in history. Monica's story reminds us that loving enough to speak also means loving enough to wait.

Speaking with Wisdom and Gentleness

Scripture does not call believers to force conversations, but to remain ready.

Peter offers wise guidance:

"Always be ready to give a defense to everyone who asks you a reason for the hope that is in you, with meekness and fear." (1 Peter 3:15, NKJV)

Meekness matters. Respect matters. Listening matters.

Often, the most meaningful conversations begin not with answers, but with questions. Taking time to understand someone's doubts, fears, or experiences communicates care and builds trust.

When words come, they do not need to be polished. A simple testimony of how Christ has changed your life can touch hearts more deeply than arguments ever could.

When Words Are Not Received

Not every conversation will end with agreement or interest. Some family members may resist or dismiss the message. Scripture prepares us for this reality.

Paul reminds us:

"*I planted, Apollos watered, but God gave the increase.*" (1 Corinthians 3:6, NKJV)

Our responsibility is faithfulness, not outcomes.

Sometimes our role is to quietly plant seeds through prayer, kindness, and consistent witness, trusting God to bring growth in His time.

Faith Lived Before It Is Spoken

Words have more impact when they are backed by a life of integrity. Family and friends see if faith results in humility, patience, forgiveness, and love.

Paul encourages believers:

"Walk in wisdom toward those who are outside." (Colossians 4:5, NKJV)

Authentic faith isn't about perfection; it's about transformation. Acknowledging failures, seeking forgiveness, and striving to grow demonstrate God's grace powerfully.

The Quiet Strength of Prayer

Behind every meaningful witness to family and friends is prayer.

Paul urges believers to pray for all people (1 Timothy 2:1). Prayer softens hearts, opens doors, and sustains hope when visible change is slow.

Some prayers are answered quickly, while others take years. Prayer helps us stay faithful during the wait.

Trusting God with What We Cannot Control

Loving enough to speak does not mean taking responsibility for someone else's choice. Salvation belongs to God. Our role is to obey out of love.

Jesus never pressured people into belief. He invited them, spoke the truth, and trusted the Father.

We are called to do the same.

A Gentle Invitation Forward

This chapter is not a call to force conversations or strain relationships. It is an invitation to trust God with your love for those closest to you.

Your presence, prayers, and words spoken with humility and grace all hold significance.

God has placed you in relationships that only you can fulfill. Through your faithfulness, He might be quietly working in ways you haven't yet seen. Every believer is a missionary, and often, the most important mission field starts at home.

Reflection Questions
1. Why do you think sharing faith with family and close friends often feels more difficult than sharing with strangers?
2. 2. What fears most commonly prevent you from talking about Christ with those you love?
3. 3. How does Scripture reshape your understanding of how love and truth work together?
4. 4. Is there someone God might be calling you to pray for more intentionally?
5. 5. What small, wise step can you take toward faithful obedience in this area??

Prayer

Father God, thank You for the people You have placed closest to us. You know our love for them and our fears as well. Grant us wisdom, patience, and courage to speak when You prompt us and to wait when You ask us to trust. Teach us to love deeply, pray faithfully, and walk humbly before You. We place our family and friends into Your hands, trusting You to work in ways we cannot see. Use our lives to reflect Your grace and truth. In Jesus' name, Amen.

Chapter 6

Shining where you are
Christ at Work and in the Neighborhood

In the previous chapter, we considered the bravery it takes to talk about Christ with those closest to us, such as family members and close friends. These relationships are very important, and being obedient in them often needs patience, prayer, and wisdom. But the call of the Great Commission doesn't end at our homes. It naturally reaches out to the places where we spend most of our time: our workplaces, neighborhoods, schools, and communities.

For most believers, life unfolds in everyday spaces. Mornings start with familiar routines. Days are spent at work, school, or home. Evenings are filled with responsibilities, conversations, and quiet moments of rest. These rhythms may seem distant from what we often think of as "mission," but Scripture shows that God loves to work in these same places.

The workplace, neighborhood, classroom, and marketplace are not distractions from the Great Commission. They are often where it is meant to be lived out.

Jesus never suggested that following Him required leaving everyday life behind. Instead, He consistently entered ordinary spaces and transformed them with His presence.

Jesus in Everyday Places

Much of Jesus' ministry took place outside religious buildings. He taught by the sea, in people's homes, along roads, and at dinner tables. He met people where they already were.

Fishermen were called while fishing. A tax collector was called while sitting at his booth. Jesus entered ordinary lives and shifted them around the kingdom of God.

Later, He told His followers:

"You are the light of the world... Let your light so shine before men, that they may see your good works and glorify your Father in heaven." (Matthew 5:14–16, NKJV)

Light does not attract attention to itself; it shows what is already present. Similarly, believers are called to reveal God's character through faithful presence.

The Mission Field We Often Overlook

Many Christians still believe that mission begins elsewhere, in another country, culture, or setting. Yet, Scripture repeatedly emphasizes that God intentionally places His people.

Paul told the Athenians:

"From one man He made all the nations, that they should inhabit the whole earth, and has determined their preappointed times and the boundaries of their dwellings." (Acts 17:26, NKJV)

This means your workplace, neighborhood, and community are purposeful. God has placed you among specific people for meaningful reasons. Colleagues, neighbors, classmates, and service providers may never step into a church. Still, they observe believers closely, how they speak, work, respond under pressure, and treat others. These everyday exchanges become quite powerful opportunities for witness.

Faith Lived Before It Is Spoken

In many settings, conversations about faith tend to come up later. What takes precedence is character.

Paul urged believers:

"Walk in wisdom toward those who are outside, redeeming the time." (Colossians 4:5, NKJV)

Wisdom manifests through integrity, diligence, kindness, and humility. Excelling at work, practicing honesty in business, showing patience under pressure, and displaying grace during conflict speak loudly in a skeptical world.

This does not mean believers hide their faith. It means faith is demonstrated before it is explained.

When people see consistency between belief and behavior, curiosity often arises.

A *Living Example: Eric Liddell*

Eric Liddell (1902–1945) provides a powerful example of faith lived openly in everyday settings. An Olympic athlete, Liddell believed his talents were gifts from God, entrusted to him for God's glory.

He famously said:

"God made me fast. And when I run, I feel His pleasure."

Liddell honored God not only through his words but also through the way he lived, competed, and treated others. Later, he served as a missionary in China, where he taught and cared for others with humility and love.

Even those who did not share his faith deeply respected him. His life reminds us that faith expressed through vocation can open doors that words alone may never reach.

Speaking with Grace When Time Is Right

While actions are important, Scripture never separates living faithfully from speaking faithfully. The two go hand in hand.

Paul writes:

"Let your speech always be with grace, seasoned with salt, that you may know how you ought to answer each one." (Colossians 4:6, NKJV)

Grace-filled speech is timely, gentle, and attentive. Conversations about faith often start naturally through questions, shared struggles, or moments of crisis. When such opportunities arise, believers do not need to feel pressure to have perfect answers. Honest testimony about what Christ has done in your life often speaks more clearly than carefully crafted explanations.

Being Present, Not Preachy

One of the greatest gifts believers can give to their communities is showing up with genuine presence: listening without judgment, serving without expecting anything in return, and showing real interest in others' lives. Jesus often asked questions before giving answers. He noticed people, listened carefully, and engaged meaningfully. Being present helps build trust, and over time, trust opens hearts.

Mission isn't about turning every interaction into a sermon; it's about being consistently available to God in everyday moments.

Holding Truth with Humility

Living faithfully in public spaces does not mean blending in or hiding convictions. It means holding truth with humility and courage.

Peter encourages believers:

"Having a good conscience, that when they defame you as evildoers, those who revile your good conduct in Christ may be ashamed." (1 Peter 3:16, NKJV)

A life shaped by Christ can stand out. Sometimes, that difference raises questions; other times, it encounters resistance. Either way, faithfulness stays the goal.

Neighbors as Sacred Opportunities

Jesus redefined "neighbor" as anyone we meet who needs love, mercy, and truth. Neighborhoods are sacred spaces where lives cross paths every day.

Simple acts of kindness, such as hospitality, assistance, and companionship, build bridges. Shared meals, conversations, and care foster relationships where faith can be shared naturally.

Jesus said:

"By this all will know that you are My disciples, if you have love for one another." (John 13:35, NKJV)

Love gives credibility to the message we carry.

Ordinary Faithfulness, Eternal Impact

Most believers will never preach to crowds or travel widely. Yet Scripture and history show that God delights in using ordinary faithfulness to accomplish extraordinary purposes.

Paul reminds us:

"Whatever you do, do it heartily, as to the Lord and not to men." (Colossians 3:23, NKJV)

When work, relationships, and daily life are offered to God, they become acts of worship—and opportunities for witness.

Trusting God with the Results

Living missionally at work and in the neighborhood requires patience. Not every seed grows quickly. Some conversations take years to bear fruit.

Paul's words offer comfort:

"I planted, Apollos watered, but God gave the increase." (1 Corinthians 3:6, NKJV)

Our role is faithfulness. God handles the outcome.

A Gentle Call Forward

This chapter is not a call to dramatic change, but to intentional presence. You do not need to leave your job, move away, or become someone else.

God is already working where you are. As you live with integrity, speak with grace, and love consistently, your everyday life becomes a testimony of God's extraordinary grace. Every believer is a missionary, not only in distant places but also in daily life. May we learn to shine quietly, faithfully, and courageously right where God has placed us.

Reflection Questions

1. In what everyday places (work, school, neighborhood, community) has God already positioned you to be a witness?
2. How do your words, attitudes, and work habits reflect Christ to those around you?
3. Why do you think "presence" and consistent character often open doors for the gospel more effectively than words alone?
4. Are there situations where you sense God inviting you to speak more openly about your faith, but you have hesitated?

5. What is one practical way you can live more intentionally for Christ in your daily routines this week?

Prayer

Lord Jesus, thank You for placing us exactly where we are. Thank You that our workplaces, neighborhoods, and daily routines are not accidents, but part of Your design. Help us to live with integrity, humility, and love, so that others may see Your character reflected in us. Give us wisdom to know when to speak and courage to respond when You open the door. Teach us to be faithful in ordinary moments, trusting You to use our lives for eternal purposes. May we shine quietly and consistently for Your glory, right where You have placed us. In Your name we pray, Amen.

Chapter 7
Courage over Fear
*Overcoming Silence and Spiritual
Apathy*

In the previous chapter, we examined what it means to live faithfully in everyday places like work, neighborhoods, and daily routines. We recognized that God often works quietly through presence, integrity, and love long before words are spoken. Many believers already live faithfully in these spaces, reflecting Christ through their actions and character.

Yet even when we desire to live this way, something often holds us back from taking the next step. That barrier is rarely a lack of belief or love. More often, it is fear. Fear quietly influences how visible our faith becomes. It affects us when we speak and when we remain silent. It determines whether we respond to a prompting from the Holy Spirit or quietly set it aside. Over time, if left unchallenged, fear can gradually turn sincere faith into hesitant silence.

This chapter encourages us to honestly examine fear, not to judge ourselves, but to understand it. Scripture doesn't call believers to panic or feel pressured, but to show courage. Not dramatic bravery, but steady, Spirit-led obedience in the face of very real human fears.

The Subtle Power of Fear

Fear rarely makes itself known loudly. More often, it sounds sensible and responsible. It urges us to wait for a better time, avoid awkward situations, protect relationships, or stay quiet until we feel more ready.

For many believers, fear appears in familiar ways:

- Fear of rejection or ridicule
- Fear of being misunderstood or labelled
- Fear of harming relationships
- Fear of not knowing what to say

These fears are very human. Even Jesus' followers faced fear. After Jesus' crucifixion, they hid behind locked doors not because they stopped believing, but because fear overtook them (John 20:19).

But fear was never meant to have the last word.

Paul reminds Timothy:

"For God has not given us a spirit of fear, but of power and of love and of a sound mind." (2 Timothy 1:7, NKJV)

Fear does not originate from God. Instead, power, love, and wisdom do.

When Fear Turns into Spiritual Apathy

Fear does not always cause open disobedience. More often, it causes a delay. We plan to speak someday. We intend to pray more intentionally later. We believe there will be another opportunity.

Over time, repeated delays can slowly turn into apathy.

Spiritual apathy is not a rejection of faith—it is a dulling of urgency. We still believe. We still attend church. We still affirm truth. But our hearts are no longer stirred by the spiritual condition of those around us.

Jesus warned against this condition when He spoke to the church in Ephesus:

"Nevertheless, I have this against you, that you have left your first love." (Revelation 2:4, NKJV)

The church had not abandoned truth or discipline, but love had cooled. Passion had faded. The fire that once compelled action had grown dim.

Apathy is dangerous because it feels safe.

Jesus and the Call to Courage

Jesus never expected His followers to be fearless. Instead, He continually calls them to be courageous.

Again and again, He says, "Do not be afraid." When Peter steps out of the boat, fear eventually overtakes him, but Jesus does not rebuke Peter for trying. He reaches out and lifts him when fear takes over (Matthew 14:29–31). Peter's failure does not cancel his obedience; it shows his humanity. Biblical courage is not the absence of fear. It is obedience in spite of fear.

Courage Comes from the Holy Spirit

Jesus never expected believers to rely solely on their own strength to live courageously. Before sending His disciples into the world, He gave them a promise:

"But you shall receive power when the Holy Spirit has come upon you; and you shall be witnesses to Me..." (Acts 1:8, NKJV)

Notice the order: power first, then witness. The courage to speak, live, and love faithfully comes from the Holy Spirit's presence, not from personality, confidence, or experience. When believers depend on the Spirit, courage quietly grows stronger over time.

A Real Example: Brother Andrew

A powerful example of courage shaped by obedience is Brother Andrew (1928–2022), often known as "God's Smuggler." Brother Andrew did not see himself as fearless.

In fact, he freely admitted his fears. Still, he believed that obedience was more important than comfort. During the Cold War, he carried Bibles into countries where Christianity was restricted or banned. As he approached border crossings, fear would rise in his heart.

Instead of turning around, he prayed simple prayers, trusting God to intervene. God repeatedly answered those prayers.

Brother Andrew's courage was not dramatic; it was faithful. He trusted God step by step, and through his obedience, many believers were strengthened and encouraged. His life reminds us that God does not work through fearlessness but through willingness.

Courage Begins with Small Steps

Many believers assume courage requires dramatic action. But Scripture often shows courage beginning with small steps of obedience.

A quiet word.

An honest answer.

An offer of prayer.

A personal testimony.

Jesus said:

"He *who is faithful in what is least is faithful also in much.*" (Luke 16:10, NKJV)

Small acts of obedience help the heart trust God more deeply.

Renewing the Mind

Fear and apathy often take hold of the mind. Scripture calls believers to renew their thinking.

Paul writes:

"*Do not be conformed to this world but be transformed by the renewing of your mind.*" (Romans 12:2, NKJV)

When we begin to see people as God sees them, eternal, loved, and valuable, fear begins to lose its grip. Perspective reshapes priorities.

Remembering What Truly Matters

Fear increases when we focus on ourselves, but courage develops when we focus on Christ.

Jesus said:

"*Whoever desires to save his life will lose it, but whoever loses his life for My sake will find it.*" (Matthew 16:25, NKJV)

This is not an appeal to recklessness but to maintaining an eternal perspective. Short-term discomfort is minor in comparison to eternal hope.

Stirring the Heart Again

Paul encouraged Timothy:

"Therefore, I remind you to stir up the gift of God which is in you." (2 Timothy 1:6, NKJV)

Spiritual fire does not always burn on its own. Sometimes it must be stirred through prayer, reflection, and renewed obedience.

Honest questions help awaken the heart:

- Where have I become comfortable?
- Where have I chosen silence instead of obedience?
- Who might God be inviting me to love more courageously?

God responds graciously to such prayers.

From Fear to Faithful Presence

Courage doesn't promise instant results, but it transforms the believer. When courage replaces fear, faith reemerges. Expectation comes back. Love deepens. Prayer becomes purposeful.

Paul reminds us:

"Therefore, my beloved brethren, be steadfast, immovable, always abounding in the work of the Lord, knowing that your labor is not in vain in the Lord." (1 Corinthians 15:58, NKJV)

No act of obedience is wasted.

A Gentle Call to Wakefulness

This chapter is not meant to pressure, but to invite. Fear is real, but it does not have to rule. Apathy may have crept in, but it does not have to stay.

God gently awakens hearts.

Every believer is a missionary, not because they are fearless, but because they are empowered by the Holy Spirit. As we learn to choose courage over fear, may our faith become visible again, not through loudness, but through loving obedience. And may God use our small, faithful steps to bring hope to those around us.

Reflection Questions
1.   What fears most often influence whether you speak or remain silent about your faith?
2.   In what ways might fear or comfort have gradually turned into spiritual apathy in your life?
3.   How does Scripture challenge the idea that courage requires fearlessness?
4.   Where do you feel the Holy Spirit prompting you to take a small step of obedience?
5.   What would it look like to trust God more fully with the outcomes of your faithfulness??

Prayer

Lord God, You know our fears, hesitations, and the spots where our hearts quiet down. Thank You that You don't condemn us but gently call us forward. Replace fear with faith and apathy with love. Fill us anew with Your Holy Spirit, giving us power, wisdom, and courage to obey. Teach us to take small steps of faith, trusting You with the outcome. May our lives reflect Your grace and truth as we choose courage over fear. In Jesus' name, Amen.

Chapter 8
Faithful until the End
Living as Witnesses in the Last Days

In the previous chapter, we faced an honest challenge: fear and spiritual apathy can quietly silence even sincere believers. We were reminded that courage is not the absence of fear, but obedience empowered by the Holy Spirit. Yet once believers begin choosing courageous speaking, when prompted, living visibly, and trusting God with outcomes, another question naturally arises:

What does faithfulness look like over time?

Sharing the gospel once might feel doable, but living as a steady witness year after year can be much more challenging. Some conversations seem to bring results quickly, while others go nowhere. Some prayers are answered fast; others take decades. Over time, discouragement can quietly sneak in, tempting believers to judge faithfulness based on visible results.

Scripture consistently reminds us of this truth. Instead of portraying a quick thrill, it carefully prepares believers for a lengthy journey characterized by perseverance rather than constant excitement. Jesus did not invite His followers to fleeting enthusiasm but to remain faithful until the very end.

Living with the End in View
The Bible frequently mentions "the last days." This phrase is intended not to cause fear or speculation, but to offer perspective. It serves as a reminder to believers that history is progressing toward God's designated end and that our lives are part of a much bigger story.

Jesus said:

"And this gospel of the kingdom will be preached in all the world as a witness to all the nations, and then the end will come." (Matthew 24:14, NKJV)

These words inspire believers with a sense of responsibility and hope. The mission goes on, and God stays firmly in control. Living with the end in mind doesn't mean constantly looking to the sky; it means approaching each day with purpose, awareness, and hope.

Faithfulness Matters More Than Visibility

In a world that values results, numbers, and recognition, Scripture presents a different standard: faithfulness.

Paul reminds us:

"Moreover, it is required in stewards that one be found faithful." (1 Corinthians 4:2, NKJV)

Faithfulness often manifests quietly through consistent prayer, patient love, gentle truth-telling, and daily obedience. Some believers sow seeds they might never see sprout, while others nurture seeds planted long ago. Ultimately, only God causes growth. This understanding relieves us of the pressure to produce visible results and directs our hearts toward faithful, steady obedience.

Jesus' Call to Persevere

Jesus openly discussed the difficulties of following Him. While He did not guarantee an easy path, He did assure followers that it would be meaningful.

"He who endures to the end shall be saved." (Matthew 24:13, NKJV)

Endurance in Scripture is about hopeful perseverance rather than grim determination. It involves choosing to stay faithful even when progress is slow or opposition appears.

Jesus often used simple images to illustrate faithfulness: servants waiting for their master, watchful stewards, lamps kept burning. These pictures remind us that the Christian life is a long journey, not a sprint, but built on trust.

When Discouragement Creeps In

Even devout believers go through periods of discouragement. Loved ones may drift away from God. Prayers can feel unanswered, and opportunities might seem to disappear rather than appear. Scripture recognizes this challenge, as the Psalms are full of sincere questions and yearning. Faith does not ignore hardship; instead, it honestly presents it to God.

Paul encouraged weary believers:

"And let us not grow weary while doing good, for in due season we shall reap if we do not lose heart." (Galatians 6:9, NKJV)

The promise is not an instant harvest, but one that comes in its due season. Faithfulness trusts God's timing, even when results are not visible.

Life of Perseverance: William Carey

One of the clearest examples of long-term dedication is William Carey (1761–1834), often regarded as the father of modern missions.

Carey spent many years in India with limited visible success. He encountered cultural obstacles, personal grief, opposition, and periods of profound discouragement. For a long time, it seemed his efforts yielded little.

Nevertheless, Carey stayed committed. He once straightforwardly stated, "I can plod." He believed consistent obedience was more important than immediate results.

Gradually, his work laid the groundwork that influenced mission work for generations. Carey's life teaches us that God frequently employs quiet persistence to bring about enduring change.

Living as Witnesses, Not Judges

In tough times, frustration can increase, especially when people oppose the gospel. Scripture encourages believers to adopt a different attitude.

Paul writes:

"Now then, we are ambassadors for Christ." (2 Corinthians 5:20, NKJV)

Ambassadors represent their King faithfully, even when the message is not welcomed. They do not force agreement; they offer an invitation. Living as witnesses means trusting God with people's responses while remaining loving, patient, and available.

Hope Anchors Faithfulness

Faithfulness is sustained by hope.

The writer of Hebrews describes hope as *"an anchor of the soul"* (Hebrews 6:19). This hope is not wishful thinking—it is rooted in the certainty of Christ's return and the fulfillment of God's promises.

Jesus assured His disciples:

"And lo, I am with you always, even to the end of the age." (Matthew 28:20, NKJV)

We do not walk this journey alone. Christ's presence accompanies us in every conversation, every prayer, and every season of waiting.

Small Acts with Eternal Weight

Scripture consistently affirms that what appears small to us matters greatly to God. Jesus observed cups of cold water, quiet prayers, and unseen acts of obedience.

Paul reminds us:

"Therefore, my beloved brethren, be steadfast, immovable, always abounding in the work of the Lord, knowing that your labor is not in vain in the Lord." (1 Corinthians 15:58, NKJV)

Faithfulness has eternal significance even when it feels ordinary.

Living Ready, Not Rushed

Jesus urged His followers to be prepared, not rushed. To stay alert, attentive, and responsive to God's guidance.

"Blessed are those servants whom the master, when he comes, will find watching." (Luke 12:37, NKJV)

Readiness is cultivated through daily faithfulness in prayer, Scripture, obedience, and love.

A Steady Call Forward

This chapter encourages us not to do more, but to stay faithful, continue walking, loving, and trusting God with what we cannot see. The world may feel uncertain, opposition might grow, and results could be slow, yet the call remains. Every believer is a lifelong missionary. As we faithfully witness during the days God gives us, may our lives quietly lead others to Christ. And let us find peace in knowing that God is faithful to finish the work He has started.

Reflection Questions

1. What does faithfulness look like in your current season of life, even if results are not visible?
2. Where have you felt discouraged or tempted to measure success by outcomes rather than obedience?
3. How does viewing your life through an eternal perspective reshape your priorities and expectations?
4. Who might God be calling you to continue loving, praying for, or witnessing to with patience?
5. What helps you remain hopeful and steady when progress feels slow?

Prayer

Faithful God, thank You for calling us not to visible success, but to steady obedience. When we feel weary or discouraged, remind us that You see every prayer, every act of love, and every quiet step of faithfulness. Help us trust Your timing and remain hopeful as we wait for You to work. Strengthen our hearts to endure with patience, humility, and joy. May our lives remain faithful witnesses to Your grace until the day we see You face to face. In Jesus' name, Amen.

Chapter 9

Beyond Borders
God's Heart for All People

In the previous chapter, we reflected on what it means to stay faithful over time by continuing to love, pray, and witness even when results are slow or unseen. We were reminded that God judges faithfulness not by visible success but by consistent obedience. Living with endurance strengthens our faith and shapes our character.

Yet, as believers learn to walk this path of long-term faithfulness, something quietly begins to change within us. Our vision starts to shift and grow clearer, expand.

Faithfulness in our current location does not diminish our hearts; instead, it expands them. As we become more rooted in obedience within our families, workplaces, and neighborhoods, we start to realize that God's purposes extend well beyond our immediate environment. The Great Commission is not limited to our daily borders. It pushes us outward into unfamiliar cultures, languages, and territories, reflecting God's boundless love for all people.

This broader perspective is not meant to divert us from focusing on local obedience. Instead, it enriches it with greater significance. Recognizing that God's love extends to every nation, we can see our daily faithfulness as a piece of a larger story—one that encompasses multiple generations, cultures, and the entire world.

God's Heart Has Always Been Global

From the start of Scripture, God's plan of redemption has always extended beyond a single people group. While He selected Israel for a particular purpose, His ultimate goal was to bless all nations through them.

God said to Abraham:

"In you all the families of the earth shall be blessed." (Genesis 12:3, NKJV)

This promise reveals the missionary heart of God. Israel was never meant to be the final destination of God's blessing, but the channel through which that blessing would flow.

The Psalms echo this global vision:

"Let the peoples praise You, O God; let all the peoples praise You." (Psalm 67:5, NKJV)

The prophets looked forward to a day when God's salvation would extend beyond Israel's borders. Isaiah proclaimed:

"I will also give You as a light to the Gentiles, that You should be My salvation to the ends of the earth." (Isaiah 49:6, NKJV)

Long before Jesus gave the Great Commission, God had already revealed His heart for all people.

Jesus and the Nations

When Jesus came, He primarily lived and ministered among the Jewish people. Yet even within that focus, He consistently pointed beyond it. He crossed cultural boundaries, spoke with outsiders, and welcomed those others avoided.

He healed the servant of a Roman centurion.

He spoke with a Samaritan woman.

He praised the faith of Gentiles.

These moments were not accidents. They were glimpses of the global mission that would soon be fully revealed.

After His resurrection, Jesus made the scope unmistakably clear:

"Go therefore and make disciples of all the nations." (Matthew 28:19, NKJV)

The word 'nations' refers not just to political states but also to peoples, ethnic groups, cultures, languages, and communities. The gospel was never meant to stay confined.

From Jerusalem to the Ends of the Earth

The book of Acts illustrates how this worldwide mission developed gradually.
Jesus told His disciples:

"You shall be witnesses to Me in Jerusalem, and in all Judea and Samaria, and to the end of the earth." (Acts 1:8, NKJV)

The pattern is significant. The mission starts locally and then expands outward. Faithfulness in Jerusalem leads to witnessing in Judea. Judea leads to Samaria. Samaria leads to the nations.

God did not ask the early believers to leave where they were. He told them to be faithful there and then follow Him as He opened doors beyond.

This same pattern continues today.

Global Mission Is Not Only "Out There"

For many Christians, the word 'missions' still evokes images of distant countries and cross-cultural travel. While those who are called to go play a vital role, Scripture never implies that global mission is exclusive to those who leave home.

In today's world, cultures intersect daily. Cities are shaped by migration. Workplaces, universities, and neighborhoods bring together people from many nations and backgrounds. In many places, the nations have already come to us. Paul reminded the Athenians:

"He has determined their preappointed times and the boundaries of their dwellings." (Acts 17:26, NKJV)

This implies that God has purposefully placed people and believers in their current positions. Your environment, community, and relationships are not accidental; they are part of God's plan. Global mission often starts with awareness, recognizing those around us not just as neighbors or colleagues but as individuals profoundly loved by God.

Supporting, Sending, and Going

Although not every believer is called to cross cultures physically, all believers are called to participate in God's global mission.

Some are called to go.

Some are called to send.

Some are called to support.

All are called to pray.

The Church functions as one body. When one part suffers, the whole body is affected. Paul described this unity beautifully when he thanked the Philippian church for sharing in his ministry through prayer and support (Philippians 1:5).

Active engagement in global mission includes:

• Praying consistently for missionaries and unreached groups
• Giving generously to support evangelistic efforts
• Inviting people from different cultures into your life
• Supporting and encouraging those called to mission work

None of these roles is insignificant.

Everyone is important.

A Life that Reflected God's Global Heart: Amy Carmichael

Amy Carmichael (1867–1951) exemplifies a deep dedication to God's compassion for all people. She spent more than fifty years in India, caring for children rescued from exploitation. Amy immersed herself in the culture by learning the language, adopting local customs, and living among those she helped. Her efforts were characterized not by immediate results but by persistent obedience and sacrificial love.

She once wrote, "One can give without loving, but one cannot love without giving." Amy's life exemplifies that a global mission is rooted in love—love that listens, learns, and serves patiently.

One Mission, Many Callings

As the book has emphasized from the beginning, the Great Commission is not about turning every believer into the same kind of missionary. It is about shaping every believer with the same heart.

Some believers dedicate their whole lives quietly serving in one place, while others travel across borders. Some offer support from afar. God unites all these callings into a single mission. Paul writes:

"There are diversities of gifts, but the same Spirit." (1 Corinthians 12:4, NKJV)

Unity does not require uniformity. Faithfulness looks different in different lives, but the mission remains the same.

Seeing Your Life in the Larger Story

Understanding God's global heart helps believers see their lives differently. Our prayers connect us to believers around the world. Our giving supports work we may never see. Our obedience becomes part of a story much larger than ourselves.

Scripture offers a glimpse of the final outcome:

"A great multitude which no one could number, of all nations, tribes, peoples, and tongues, standing

before the throne and before the Lamb." (Revelation 7:9, NKJV)

This is the direction history is heading.

Every faithful act, whether local or global, brings us closer to that moment.

Faithful Where You Are, Open to Where God Leads

This chapter does not urge you to abandon your responsibilities or feel guilty about staying put. Instead, it encourages you to hold your life loosely and openly.

Stay faithful where God has placed you.

Be attentive to His guidance. Be willing to support His work beyond your borders.

God may never require you to travel widely geographically, but He will ask you to love generously, pray earnestly, and care genuinely. Every believer is a missionary not because they physically go somewhere, but because they are part of God's mission.

As we faithfully live out our daily lives, let's keep our hearts open to the vastness of God's love. And let's take joy in knowing that our obedience, no matter where it takes us, has eternal significance.

Reflection Questions

1. How has your understanding of God's heart for all nations grown as you have read this chapter?
2. In what ways has God already connected your life to people from different cultures or backgrounds?
3. What role might God be inviting you to play in His global mission—going, supporting, praying, or encouraging others?
4. How does seeing your life as part of God's larger story change the way you view your daily faithfulness?
5. What is one practical step you can take to remain open and responsive to God's work beyond your immediate surroundings?

Prayer

God of all nations, thank You that Your love reaches every people, culture, and language. Thank You for inviting us into a mission that is far greater than ourselves. Help us remain faithful where You have placed us, while keeping our hearts open to Your work around the world. Teach us to pray broadly, give generously, and love sincerely. Use our lives near and far for Your glory. May we rejoice in knowing that our obedience today echoes into eternity. In Jesus' name, Amen.

Chapter 10

Living a Legacy of Mission

In the previous chapter, we lifted our eyes beyond our immediate surroundings to see God's heart for all people. We were reminded that the Great Commission extends across cultures, generations, and borders, and that every believer has a role in God's global mission. Yet as our vision expands, a deep personal question naturally arises.

What will remain after us?

Every follower of Christ leaves a legacy. The question is not *whether* we will leave one, but *what kind* of legacy it will be. Long after our words fade and our routines end, our lives continue to speak through the people we have influenced, the faith we have modeled, and the obedience we have lived out.

Living a legacy of mission means choosing each day to invest our lives in ways that last, shaping people, families, churches, and future generations for the gospel's sake.

At the core of this legacy is discipleship.

Passing Faith Forward

Jesus' command has never changed:

"Go therefore and make disciples of all nations... teaching them to observe all things that I have commanded you." (Matthew 28:19–20, NKJV)

The Great Commission isn't just about reaching those who don't yet know Christ; it's also about forming them. Discipleship ensures the mission continues long after our own journey is over.

The next generation is not merely the future of the Church; it is also its present. Young people are already shaping culture, influencing society, and asking deep questions about meaning and truth. Investing in them today prepares them to carry the gospel forward tomorrow.

Discipleship goes beyond simply passing on information; it's about shaping lives. Young believers learn what it truly means to follow Jesus not only through our teachings but also through how we demonstrate prayer, forgiveness, service, perseverance, and love.

Often, our actions demonstrate more effectively than our words do.

Intentional Formation, Not Accidental Faith

A missional legacy is never accidental; it is built with purpose. Effective discipleship relies on relationships. It develops through trust, shared experiences, and consistent presence. When young people feel seen, valued, and loved, they become receptive to spiritual guidance.

Grounding them in Scripture is vital. Biblical literacy prepares believers to recognize truth, handle pressure, and live faithfully in a confusing world. But teaching must go beyond theory. Young disciples need help connecting biblical truth to real decisions, struggles, and questions.

Involving them in service and mission is equally important. Faith grows when it is practiced. Local outreach, community service, and cross-cultural experiences help young believers see that the gospel is active and outward-focused.

Leadership development also plays a vital role. When young believers are trusted with responsibility, they grow in confidence, ownership, and commitment. Preparing them to lead ensures continuity and faithfulness in the mission.

The Church and the Home Working Together

The local church plays a crucial role in shaping missional legacy. Strong children's and youth ministries should do more than entertain; they should equip young people for **lifelong faith**.

Families are vital to this process. Parents are the primary teachers of their children, and the church's role is to support, encourage, and equip them. When church and homework are combined, discipleship is reinforced, and faith becomes a regular part of daily life.

Intergenerational relationships strengthen the body of Christ. Older believers provide wisdom, perspective, and testimony. Younger believers offer energy, questions, and vision. When generations learn from each other, the Church grows in unity and depth.

Creating spaces for spiritual growth, such as small groups, Bible studies, retreats, and mission opportunities, supports young believers in developing a missional worldview and building a resilient faith.

Timothy: A Faith Handed Down

A powerful biblical example of missional legacy is found in Timothy, Paul's young co-worker in the gospel. Paul reminds him:

"When I call to remembrance the genuine faith that is in you, which dwelt first in your

grandmother Lois and your mother Eunice." (2 Timothy 1:5, NKJV)

Timothy's faith did not develop in isolation. It was nurtured at home, strengthened through mentorship, and activated through mission. Paul deeply invested in Timothy by teaching, encouraging, correcting, and entrusting him with leadership.

As a result, Timothy became a dedicated pastor and missionary leader, spreading the gospel to others.

His life teaches us that a legacy is seldom created by a single dramatic event. Instead, it is shaped through consistent effort, dedicated instruction, and a loving example over the years.

Influence That Outlives Us

Living a legacy of mission is about influence, not recognition.

A character that leaves a deeper impression than mere visibility. Values like integrity, humility, and love influence lives long after the memory of accomplishments fades. Faithful service, whether in public or behind the scenes, leaves a lasting legacy. Relationships are profoundly significant. Showing compassion and grace in our investments in people fosters environments where growth and transformation thrive.

Mentoring, sharing wisdom, and journeying with others amplify our impact across generations.

Paul understood this well when he wrote:

"The things that you have heard from me among many witnesses, commit these to faithful men who will be able to teach others also." (2 Timothy 2:2, NKJV)

This is the legacy multiplied.

Practical Ways to Build a Missional Legacy

Some legacies are written; others are lived.

Teaching, mentoring, and storytelling pass faith along. Faithful documentation, whether through writing, teaching, or testimony, can inspire future generations.

Strong communities enhance their legacy. Churches and families that foster trust, prayer, and encouragement build environments where missions flourish.

Excellence and integrity in everyday duties also matter. A life lived consistently before God and others serves as a strong testimony.

Above all, example shapes legacy. A life marked by faith, perseverance, humility, and love becomes a living sermon.

The Ripple Effect of Faithfulness

Faithful service produces ripples that reach far beyond what we can see.

Disciplining a single person can influence generations. Investing in a few can change communities. Obedience in one place can resonate across the world.

When believers empower others to lead, teach, and serve, the ripple effect grows. Building on the foundation set by those before us honors their legacy and passes it on.

Living with Eternity in View

The ultimate legacy of a mission is not programs, buildings, or titles. It is lives transformed by the gospel.
Each act of obedience is significant. Every prayer is meaningful. Each faithful step holds eternal importance. Scripture teaches us:

"Therefore, my beloved brethren, be steadfast, immovable, always abounding in the work of the Lord, knowing that your labor is not in vain in the Lord." (1 Corinthians 15:58, NKJV)

As we live with an eternal perspective, our lives become integrated into God's ongoing story, which continues until Christ's return.

Living missionally means living with eternity in mind.
To disciple others is to shape the future.

To remain faithful is to leave a legacy that points
beyond ourselves to the faithfulness of God.

89

Chapter 11

The Heart of the Christian Faith

Reiterate the Great Commission again

In the previous chapters, we explored the true meaning of making disciples: followers of Jesus who grow in obedience and faith, rather than mere converts. At the heart of this calling is one defining command given by Jesus himself. This command instructs the Church and reveals the essence of the Christian faith.

We often call it the Great Commission.

These words are not simply the final recorded teaching of Jesus before His ascension. They are a direct charge to every follower of Christ, shaping both our identity and our purpose. To understand what it means to follow Jesus, we must understand this commission not only in what it asks of us, but also in what it reveals about God.

Standing on the Mountain with the Disciples
Matthew records the moment clearly:

90

"Then the eleven disciples went away into Galilee, to the mountain which Jesus had appointed for them. When they saw Him, they worshiped Him; but some doubted. And Jesus came and spoke to them, saying, 'All authority has been given to Me in heaven and on earth. Go therefore and make disciples of all the nations, baptizing them in the name of the Father and of the Son and of the Holy Spirit, teaching them to observe all things that I have commanded you; and lo, I am with you always, even to the end of the age.' Amen." (Matthew 28:16–20, NKJV)

These verses are familiar to many believers, yet when we slow down and reflect on them carefully, we begin to notice details that are both humbling and deeply encouraging.

One detail is easy to overlook: "they worshiped Him, but some doubted."

The Great Commission was not given to a group of fearless, fully confident believers. It was given to men who sincerely worshiped Jesus, yet still wrestled with doubt. Jesus did not wait for their doubts to disappear. He did not rebuke them or withdraw the mission.

Instead, He drew near.

This should comfort every believer who feels inadequate, uncertain, or unqualified. The mission of God is built not on the strength of our faith, but on the perfection of our Savior.

"All Authority Has Been Given to Me"

Jesus begins the Great Commission with a declaration that anchors everything that follows:

"All authority has been given to Me in heaven and on earth."

Before Jesus tells His disciples what to do, He reminds them who He is.

The Church's mission does not depend on human effort, persuasive speech, or cultural influence. Rather, it is grounded in the authority of the risen Christ, which extends over every nation, culture, government, and individual.

This truth gives believers confidence. When we share the gospel, we do not speak on our own authority. We speak as ambassadors of the One who conquered sin and death. The success of the mission does not depend on us; it depends on Him.

"Go Therefore and Make Disciples"

Flowing directly from Jesus' authority is His command:

"Go therefore and make disciples..."

This is an active, outward-facing call. The word 'go' implies movement into relationships, conversations, neighborhoods, workplaces, and communities. It does not require a change of location so much as a change of posture.

As we saw earlier, making disciples involves far more than introducing someone to Christ. It means walking alongside people, teaching them to follow Jesus, and helping them grow in obedience and faith. Discipleship happens in everyday life through shared meals, prayer in times of hardship, patient teaching, and faithful example.

This command is not reserved for pastors or missionaries. You do not need a title, a pulpit, or formal training to make disciples. What you need is a willingness to obey and a heart shaped by love.

"Of All Nations"

Jesus then expands the scope of the mission: "...*of all nations.*"

From the beginning, God's plan was never limited to one group of people. The gospel is for every culture, language, and background. Scripture affirms that humanity shares a common origin, even though we express it in diverse ways (Genesis 1:26–28; Acts 17:26).

Today, this global scope feels closer than ever. People from many nations live, study, and work together. In cities and towns around the world, believers interact daily with people who have never clearly heard the gospel.

The nations have come to us.

This reality reshapes our understanding of obedience. Following Jesus does not always require crossing borders. Sometimes, it begins by paying attention to coworkers, neighbors, classmates, and friends.

Baptizing and Teaching

Jesus describes the process of disciple-making clearly:

"Baptizing them... teaching them to observe all things that I have commanded you."

Baptism publicly declares faith and identification with Christ. Teaching obedience is an ongoing journey. Faith is more than just an inner belief; it involves a transformed life guided by Jesus' teachings.

This kind of teaching requires patience, humility, and relationship. It means walking alongside others as they grow, struggle, and learn, just as someone once walked alongside us.

In this sense, every believer remains both a learner and a teacher.

"I Am with You Always"

Jesus ends the Great Commission with a promise that sustains the entire mission:

"And lo, I am with you always, even to the end of the age."

This promise turns the command into a shared journey rather than a heavy burden. We are not sent alone; Christ's presence goes with us into every conversation, classroom, hospital room, and workplace.

The same Jesus who sends us also walks with us.

Mission Woven Through Scripture

To fully understand the Great Commission, we must see it within the broader story of Scripture. God's heart for the nations did not begin in the New Testament.

God's covenant with Abraham carried a global promise:

"In you all the families of the earth shall be blessed." (Genesis 12:3, NKJV)

The prophets echoed this vision. The Psalms praise God, whose salvation is intended for all nations. Jesus realized these promises by crossing cultural boundaries and accepting outsiders.

After His ascension, the early Church embraced this calling. Empowered by the Holy Spirit, ordinary believers carried the gospel from Jerusalem to Judea, Samaria, and beyond through homes, marketplaces, and cities.

A *Living Example: Hudson Taylor*

One powerful example of living out the Great Commission is Hudson Taylor (1832–1905), founder of the China Inland Mission.

Taylor was deeply burdened by the millions in China who had never heard the gospel. At a time when missionary work was often tied to Western culture, he made a radical decision. He adopted Chinese clothing, learned the language, and lived among the people he served. He believed the gospel should be presented without unnecessary cultural barriers.

Taylor faced illness, opposition, financial uncertainty, and deep personal loss. Yet he persevered, trusting God daily. By the end of his life, thousands of missionaries had followed his example, and countless Chinese had come to faith.

His life reminds us that obedience to the Great Commission requires humility, cultural sensitivity, and complete reliance on God. God delights in using ordinary people who trust Him fully.

Embracing the Mission Personally

The Great Commission is not merely something to understand; it is something to embrace. It invites us to align our hearts with

God's heart for the world and to view our lives as channels through which His grace can flow.

Our professions, relationships, and daily routines are not obstacles to the mission. They are often the very means through which God works.

This calling is a privilege to treasure, not a burden to endure.

As we continue this journey, may we move beyond simply admiring the Great Commission and begin living it faithfully, humbly, and courageously, right where God has placed us.

Questions for Reflection

1. In what ways have you seen God's heart for all nations reflected in Scripture or in your own life?
2. Where might God be inviting you to participate more intentionally in making disciples?

Prayer

Dear Lord, thank You for the privilege of being part of Your redemptive plan. Help us to understand the Great Commission not only with our minds, but with our hearts. Align our desires with Yours, and give us courage to obey in the places You have already placed us. We trust that You are with us always. In Jesus' name, Amen.

Chapter 12
Embracing the Call

Throughout this journey, we have followed the heart of God from His personal call on each believer to His global mission for all nations, and finally to the legacy that faithful lives leave behind. In the previous chapter, we were reminded that the Great Commission doesn't end with us. It continues through the people we disciple, the faith we demonstrate, and the obedience we pass to the next generation.

However, legacy always results in a moment of choice.

Every follower of Christ eventually reaches a point where reflection must turn into action. After hearing God's heart, understanding His mission, and realizing the eternal significance of faithfulness, the question we face is no longer abstract or theoretical. It becomes deeply personal.

How will I respond to God's call?

This final chapter isn't about learning something new. It's about embracing what God has already been saying. Throughout these pages, God hasn't just been speaking to inform us but to invite us into a life of purpose, obedience, and trust. Embracing the call to mission isn't about trying harder or becoming someone else. It starts with listening carefully, responding honestly, and surrendering completely.

As we reach the conclusion of this book, the message is clear but meaningful: to pause, to reflect, and to move forward.

Chapter 13
Epilogue
A Symphony of Transformation

"Jesus did not let him, but said, 'Go home to your own people, and tell them what great things the Lord has done for you, and how He has had compassion on you.' (Mark 5:19, NKJV)

As our journey concludes, we don't reach a final ending but rather a point of listening.

What we hear is not just a single voice but a symphony. Countless lives, transformed by grace, each playing a unique note in God's great work of redemption. They're not distant legends or unreachable heroes; they're ordinary believers who understand one simple truth: when God transforms a life, He also calls it to serve.

The Great Commission does not silence individuality; it restores it. God does not eliminate our callings, talents, or personalities. He gathers them, molds them, and directs them for His purposes. Every surrendered life becomes a melody. Every faithful step joins the ongoing song of redemption.

Akiane Kramarik

Akiane Kramarik, a child prodigy and Christian artist, exemplifies creativity devoted to God. From an early age, her artwork demonstrated a deep spiritual awareness influenced by prayer and Scripture. Her most famous painting, Prince of Peace, transcended cultures, languages, and belief systems.

Akiane did not deliver sermons. However, her art serves as a testimony that invites viewers to pause, wonder, and reflect on the beauty, truth, and reality of Jesus Christ. Her life reminds us that the gospel can be shared visually, thoughtfully, and powerfully when God-given gifts are given back to Him.

William Wilberforce

William Wilberforce (1759–1833), a British member of Parliament, saw his political work as a calling from God. After a deep conversion to Christ, he dedicated his life to ending the transatlantic slave trade. For many years, he faced ridicule, resistance, and repeated political setbacks. Yet, he persisted.

Wilberforce's faith influenced his beliefs, integrity, and perseverance. His persistent effort ultimately contributed to ending slavery in the British Empire. His life reminds us that public service, when guided by the gospel, can become a sacred calling.

Florence Nightingale

Florence Nightingale (1820–1910), recognized as the founder of modern nursing, saw her work as an act of obedience to God's call. Driven by her Christian faith, she cared for the sick with dignity, compassion, and unwavering dedication.

Her mission quietly unfolded within hospital wards, policy reforms, and tireless care for the vulnerable. Through her faithfulness, the gospel was made visible in acts of mercy and healing. She reminds us of that service, when rooted in love, powerfully speaks of Christ.

Johann Heinrich Pestalozzi

Johann Heinrich Pestalozzi (1746–1827), a Christian educator, believed education should shape not only the mind but also the heart. His faith-driven approach emphasized character, compassion, and moral responsibility.

His influence helped shape modern education and reminds the Church that forming young lives is a sacred mission work whose impact stretches across generations.

George Müller

George Müller (1805–1898) never owned a restaurant, but he fed thousands. As a Christian evangelist, Müller cared for more than 10,000 orphans in England, relying entirely on prayer and God's provision.

He never publicly asked for donations. Instead, he trusted God openly, and God provided faithfully. Müller's life stands as a testimony that faith expressed through trust, hospitality, and obedience can be a powerful witness to the gospel.

The Ordinary Lives God Still Uses

Artists.

Politicians.

Caregivers.

Educators.

Business leaders.

Parents.

Grandparents.

Workers.

Neighbors.

These lives are not extraordinary because of fame, but because of faithfulness. They remind us that a mission doesn't need a title, a platform, or a passport; **it needs obedience**.

As this book comes to an end, the invitation still stands.

Your life, your vocation, your relationships, and your daily rhythms are not peripheral to God's mission. They are a part of it. The gospel advances not only through sermons and strategies but through faith lived publicly, humbly, and authentically consistently.

The Final Note

May we conclude this journey with a new perspective, viewing our lives not as isolated solos but as harmonies in God's grand symphony of redemption. May we share the gospel through both our words and actions. May we serve bravely and with kindness. May our everyday obedience be so genuine that others are inspired to turn to Christ.

And may our lives echo this enduring truth:

The gospel is not just a message we proclaim.
It is a life we live.
Every believer is a missionary.

Amen.

A Final Commissioning Prayer

May the God who called you by name,
who found you in grace and formed you in truth,
now send you with purpose and peace. May you
go where He has placed you in your home, work,
friendships, and community with eyes open to
see and a heart willing to love. Let the words of
Christ dwell in you,
the power of the Spirit strengthens you,
and the presence of the Father surround you.
When fear whispers, may faith respond. When
weariness appears, may hope persist. When
silence seems easier, may love give you courage.

May your life speak clearly of Jesus
in your kindness,
in your integrity,
in your obedience,
and in your compassion for those still searching.

And when your work feels insignificant or
unseen, may you remember that nothing done in
Jesus Christ is ever wasted.

Go now, not alone and not unprepared, but sent
by God, sustained by grace,
and confident in this promise.

*"And lo, I am with you always, even to the end of
the age."*
(Matthew 28:20, NKJV)

Go in peace.
Live faithfully.
Love boldly.

Every believer is a missionary.
Amen.

A *personal word to you*

Thank you for joining me on this journey. If you've read this far, you've dedicated your time, attention, and heart to these pages, and I truly appreciate it.

From the beginning, my prayer was simple: that this book would inspire you to see your life as meaningful and useful in God's hands, right where you are. If you find something you read stirring, challenging, or a reminder that God can work through you in everyday moments, I would love to hear about it.

Your story matters. What God is doing in your life through your home, work, and relationships can encourage others who are learning to live out the same calling.

Thank you for reading with an open heart. May God continue to guide, strengthen, and use you as you live out the Great Commission in your daily life.

With sincere gratitude,

David Vundi
Email: david@alphyschool.org

About the Author

With a lifelong commitment to Christian teaching, David Vundi encourages men and women to discover their God-given purpose and to live in faithful obedience. Guided by Scripture, his work inspires believers to see the importance of their daily lives within God's plan.

Through teaching and writing, he seeks to awaken believers from passive faith, urging them to live boldly, love deeply, and share the gospel. His message is both simple and challenging. God works through ordinary people in ordinary places to accomplish extraordinary results.

Read more from
DAVID VUNDI

Missionaries Who Changed the World
Series

www.alphy.at

Available on Amazon. Copyright © 2022 Alphy School.